smartphone empire: make money online using your smartphone

PART 1

Table Of Contents

Let's face it, for most of you reading this your cell phone is nothing more than a liability. The majority of the population has the hottest, newest smartphone but hasn't any clue how to do anything beyond sending a text message or posting a selfie on Instagram. Like Prometheus, people today are holding the fire of the gods, the tool to all possibility yet, they have no idea of its almost limitless potential. I believe the greatest tool of our century when it comes to relationship and business building is our smartphone. The personal device in your pocket has the capability to book flights, speak to anyone anywhere using both video and audio. Plus, your smartphone literally allows you to carry your business and clients in your pocket with you at all times. You can have a conference call sitting pool side or you can complete a financial transaction with someone on the other side of the planet while walking your dog. The opportunity is limitless.

 Smartphone Empire is dedicated to helping everyday people use an everyday tool to do more than play candy crush and post pictures of their food on Instagram. In this book I'll teach you the very basics on how you can use the world's favorite toy and turn it into a powerful handheld business building and money making machine.

Getting Started

Historically building a business is hard, building an online business without any guidance can be even harder. However, today we live in a very unique time. We are currently in a paradoxical revolution that makes starting a successful online business simple, yet difficult to build and maintain. Every year a new technology, a new application and a new social media platform comes and goes. The abundance of information can be overwhelming and not only confuses entrepreneurs but can cause new potential entrepreneurs to quit before they even get started. So one can imagine that starting a business or just simply making some extra cash on a smartphone may seem almost impossible. The truth is smartphones can actually simplify many of the day to day task needed to be completed, in order to either make some quick cash or building a strong sustaining income.

 Smartphones are not the answer to everything but they are almost the answer to anything needing to get done. What I love about smartphones is the simpler and wider range of applications that allow you to not only do things you can already do on your personal computer, but even things you can't do on your PC as well. It' doesn't matter what kind of smartphone you have, all the phones on the market are capable of completing the same tasks. The companies are very competitive and are always spending money and research to make their phones the best possible while maintaining an affordable price. So for the sake of your time and mine, I will not be putting a chapter on which phone you should buy. Instead I'd rather get right into the details.

Who Am I?

Last year in November 2014 I didn't have money to buy a $450-$2000 dollar computer, so I started off with a samsung Lg3 phone. The phone was given to me for free from a friend, I didn't even have a plan. The phone was literally useless without internet. I lived in my cousin's basement with a single mattress, no job, and an empty mini fridge. My only stroke of luck was an unlocked wifi connection I stole from my surrounding area. I had to literally sit by a basement window with a jacket and a winter hat to get a decent connection. I was in a slump and I knew the only way out of it was by strategy and determination. I was going to get out of this horrible situation no matter what. And I knew with limited resources I had no choice but to use only what I had, and trust me it was just a Smartphone.

In today's world anything is possible, we just need the right information, determination and education to make our dreams come true. We can build an empire with just our mobile devices and I can show you how but first you need money.

How do you get money without a job?

Welcome to level one of this program, I call it Digital hustling mode

What is Digital hustling and why not call it E- hustling mode? Well for one, it's things you can do to make some money but isn't necessarily building a business. Things such as free lance writing for blogs and other things like that is what I would call a digital hustle, a low cost means to put some cash in your pocket. Second, Digital hustling mode sounded cooler.

When you're getting your digital hustle on, you live in survival and education mode. During this phase of the game your main objective is to learn about building an online empire. Studying things like internet marketing and social media platforms, all the while making enough cash working for others online to get by. Usually a digital hustler or freelancer is a person with no 9-5 job, so they find or create opportunities online to make the cash they need. This is all apart of the game, if you can make it out of this phase in one piece you can do anything. For me it was life or death. I was spending 8 hours a day looking for a job, yet it wasn't paying off. Rent was coming and I needed to put food on the table, so I did.

Welcome to ground zero, this may be the hardest part of your journey, no skills, bad habits and limited knowledge and resources.

It's time to get your hustle on!

In this chapter I'll discuss how you can make the money you need to hold your position until you get that job you've been waiting for or replace the need for a part/full-time job completely.

What you'll need to get started

1. A smartphone of course

2. A monthly income goal

3. A wifi connection: If you need to go to Starbucks, a McDonald's or any other location that has available wifi for the public go there.

4. Patience and determination.

Chapter 1: The easiest ways to make money online using your smart phone

This chapter isn't for building a business, this chapter is for those who are in need of cash quick. We've all been there, nothing to be ashamed of.

Here is how I fed myself while I was building the empire I have today.

<u>Craigslist</u>

Craigslist, Kijji (If you're in Canada) and other similar platforms cost nothing at all. Selling Stuff on Craigslist is easy. It's also not uncommon for people to post free items you can easily scoop up and turn for profit. Sure, it requires a little more work leaving to grab things but it'll definitely help put food in your stomach during desperate times. I was able to earn roughly an extra $700 a month. This is what covered my rent for almost 6 months.

When shopping on craigslist keep a lookout for suspicious behaviour, it's not uncommon for people to attempt to rip others off and yes in the past craiglist was used for serial killers to lure their victims. Never go to sell or buy anything alone, always bring at least 1 person with you and always give the address you're visiting to a friend.

Retail Arbitrage

Some people won't like or agree with me on this method but if you're like how I was before I started building my S.P.E. (Smartphone Empire) you had no other option. And that first option for myself was retail arbitrage.

Retail arbitrage is easy and you can do it without owning a website. The reason I started retail arbitrage was simple, I had nothing of my own to sell. I literally just had a few pieces of clothing, a portable electric stove and a bicycle. Giving up either item was just out of the question. I found out about retail arbitrage from a friend who had told me about selling items of clothing, shoes, some electronics and even furniture he didn't own or pay for. This dude literally went between Ebay and amazon reposting the same items but at a higher price.

At first, I had to Post low priced items on ebay because Ebay has a policy that for the first 60 days. You have to wait a 2 week period before the money ends up into your account. Once that period was over, the money is transferred right away into your account with each purchase. Making you able to take that money, pay and send the item to your buyer. Leaving you with the difference. I was blown away by this idea so I started right away. My first week I made $100 selling a few cheap but in demand items such as toaster ovens, a few costumes and even a small dining room table that cost $21.00 which was the first item I sold by the way. 3 months later I making over $1,000 in sales.

The second option was actually quite the surprise, Freelance writing. Think about it, we're In the age of information. Everything is being recorded, written down, repackaged resold to us over and over. How similar are all the blog post, all, YouTube videos and marketing/business advice we consume everyday? We're literally begging to be told what to do by others just so that we feel like we're doing something. For all of this content addiction, freelance writers are needed. And it's extremely easy to do, I'm writing this paragraph on my smartphone right now. The requirements differ from client to client but over all you just need basic writing and grammar skills. However, the higher your skill level the more you can offer, more you offer the more you can charge for your services.

Now as you can see I don't have exact instructions on how to do be successful at retail arbitrage or freelance writing. The amount of time it would take for you to read it. It would take far less time if you searched how to be successful in these two fields on YouTube and just watch the videos on these topics. There's literally hundreds or maybe even thousands of videos out there. It's just up to you to do the damn research.

Ebay Selling Basics: If you have a printer, buy a small letter scale so you can benefit by using the self-service printing labels offered by the US Postal Service. As a Paypal and eBay customer, you get discounts on the postage of your articles without having to go to the post office! Another great thing about eBay, is that they will give you free listings each month so you can post your items for free.

To be truly successful, I recommend that you follow my rules

1. Be Upfront
If what you sell is in less-than-perfect condition, be upfront and straightforward. On eBay, the customer is valued the most, and if your buyer does not like what he/she receives, they will get their money back from you. One time I accidently damaged an item before sending it out and had to contact the buyer to inform them that their item was now damaged beyond repair and I gave them their refund. Well that didn't go over so well, that customer was so upset she wrote a negative review.

2. Snap Great Pictures

Post pictures of clothing worn by a friend or a family member, but make sure to crop out their face to keep their identity a secret. Another great way to take professional pictures for items like clothing is to purchase or make mannequins to model your clothing. You can easily learn how to build or buy your own mannequins.

3. Give correct measurements.

4. **Seller, Buyer Communication**
It's important you keep a close eye on your inbox to better communicate with sellers or potential sellers. Anything can go wrong at any given moment and it's important to stay on top of all problems. Remember those who are buying off you will rate you. And poor ratings can negatively affect your sells.

Fiver: Fiver is a unique website where people freelance their services for a minimum of $5.00 but you can potentially make much more.

For example: If you can format Microsoft word files into Kindle ebooks you can charge $5.00 per every 10-15 pages.

Another added bonus is that you can not only post multiple gigs to increase your chances of success but you can also collect tips. The better you perform the better your rating, the better your rating increases the likelihood of your sales going up.

The key to success on Fiver depend on a few things.

1.Your skills: Take a second and reflect on anything you're good at. If you're a graphic designer you can do things such as creating book covers, labels, business cards, logos, magazines, banners, facebook cover photo's you name it.

2. Unique ideas and personality: Fiver is very competitive and if you're someone from North America for example you may have a tough time competing with people from certain countries where the U.S. dollar is much more valuable compared to their home currency. This is more likely to make them much more willing to provide more value for the same or less of the price. So you have to stand out and be an individual to catch people's attention, offering unique gigs is a great way of doing so.

One individual I've recently came across on Fiver caught my eye. I don't know what his real name is but he goes by the name Jesus Christ.

Jesus Christ offers a great gig for people who produce products and content. He creates videos of himself dressed as Jesus and basically reads a script that would go something like this: "Hi, it is I, your lord and savior and I bring you a gift". This is a prime example of using your unique personality along with your unique ideas, did I mention this person is now top seller on Fiver and is fairly new to website?

Along with selling things on Fiver it's a great place to shop for pretty decent and sometimes really high quality work.

Odesk and Upworks

 These are great places to both find freelance work or freelancers to get a specific job done. On these sites you can find work or find others to work for you at a fair price doing almost anything. How this site works is that you post an ad of what kind of work you need done,negotiate a price and the first half of the payment is deposited in the escrow. If you have a freelance service to offer? Your job is to seek out these people who are looking for your help.

Chapter 2: Organization

Your Smartphone is the ultimate tool, with it you can build your empire but that's not possible without knowledge, patience, hustle and most importantly strategy. Smartphones are perfect for coming up with the best battle plan to fit your needs no matter what your goals are. There are many apps you can download that can help you stay motivated and organized, add discipline and you have the best structure for building success.

Idea's are powerful and important, but even more important is the storing and organization of ideas. You never know when a good idea can lead to gold and you definitely don't want to forget a potential Million dollar idea right? Each day I'm constantly reminded of what task, big or small that I need to accomplish. I also have my phone set up to deliver a motivational quote every hour incase I lose focus. You're often going to feel like quitting on your journey so this is an idea I highly recommend. Idea's are great but without setting goals and staying disciplined they're worthless. I also Recommend you use a calendar app to stay tight on all of your deadlines. You have to remember the convenience of your smartphone and that with it you can structure your day almost flawlessly. There is no excuse to not get work done. You can literally have it with you all day, you also can pull it out and access the internet nearly anywhere.

When it comes to task management I use two simple ways, grocery list and Team based organization. I only use these 2 methods so it's important to research different methods of managing your tasks to find what works for you.

The Checklist

The Checklist is by far the most popular task management method. You puts all the tasks needed to be completed the night before in their respective due date and times to be completed. There are dozens of apps you can use to organize your tasks. Preferably I use google keep as that's what came with my Lg3 Samsung smartphone, you can also use evernote or any other organizational app. Break up all of your ideas into categories as you go along. Have a section for book idea's, entrepreneurial ideas and even passwords for different login information. Once you've become overwhelmed with sticky notes on your app, it's best you move those idea's to whatever storage cloud service you prefer. I like taking screenshots of the my notes so the images automatically stores in the cloud, that way I can delete this information and move on.

Goal Setting

No matter which app you choose, I'm sure we can all agree that goal setting and taking action are what makes businesses successful. Using the google keep app as a checklist, you can set a daily reminder of all or individual task needing to be completed each day. I love this because nothing beats waking up everyday reminded of what great things I have to accomplish. Setting my alarm to keep track of my goals has dramatically increased my productivity. The only con is that it's not great for handling large projects but it is however excellent for tracking smaller details.

Team Based Productivity

When you're working with your team, you need a way to keep up with what everyone's working on and the progress of your team projects. Team members can add and edit tasks as well as discuss tasks within a comment thread or an instant messenger service, making group task management easy. Beyond setting due dates, tasks can often have sub-tasks and the larger projects can be organized in their own boards or lists to keep everything organized for each of your projects or clients. You can also add files to tasks, so you can keep everything needed to complete the task in one spot and share them with your other team members. Look for a great team project that works for you, I however prefer to use Freedcamp.

Freedcamp- Project Management system

Freedcamp is a project management tool and organization system. Allowing for single or multiple users to collaborate using cloud computing. The best part about it is Freedcamp is free for unlimited number of users and projects. The applications allows users to assign tasks to people, set milestones, schedule events on a calendar, use discussion boards, and track time spent on tasks. In my opinion it's the simplest and most effective management system currently out there.

How to eliminate distractions

The Smartphone is equally useful as it is distracting. With the tap of the screen we have the whole world at our fingertips. And with constant notifications, we most often get in our own way, Infact the hardest part about building a business using a smartphone is the constant distractions from random text messages and app updates. If you really intend on building a smartphone empire you're going to have to cut all that crap out, clean house completely. Getting notifications on someone else's relationship status or any other annoying crap will cost you focus, time and money. I've seen people on facebook who literally would spend hours debating, making fun off or trolling people. I'm not completely sure, but i'm almost 100% positive those people have nothing productive going in their lives at that moment. I don't think anyone realizes just how much time they are wasting on their phone, they could conquer the world but they'd rather Netflix and chill or debate the color of a dress on Twitter.

 Delete all of the apps that aren't related to your business. Never log into facebook or instagram unless you're using it to be productive. Do not respond, reply or take part in any negative comments or debates. Delete all dating applications (I know you have them) and do not even web surf unless it is necessary. The convenience of smart phones has made the majority of us addicted to the instant gratification of being able to access almost anything right away. However i've yet to see a smart phone give anyone instant success. If you're not focused, you'll literally give all your time to your smartphone and not see a single return on that time simply because you decided to use it for the destruction and not the construction of your own life.

One of things I love most is downloading apps for my smartphone. You can Literally find 1,000s of applications for your smartphone that can dramatically increase productivity and help build your business.

Here's a list I compiled of necessary applications that I use for tasks. You'll notice that I've listed 0 games or anything that has nothing to do with expanding my business.

Social/Media

Periscope
iOS / Android

By now you've heard of Periscope, Twitter's live-streaming video app. From celebrities broadcasting directly to fans to journalists reporting live from the scenes of breaking news. Periscope is a powerful tool for everyone who wants to become an entrepreneur. For those who are interested how this app operates? Check out the book Scope-School on amazon though you could most likely get this same information online for free.

Cyber Dust
iOS / Android / Windows Phone

Cyber dust is one of the most important apps business people can have. After creator of Cyber Dust (Mark Cuban) had his own private emails used against him during a lawsuit. Mark decided something needed to be done about the poor level of privacy when doing business in our digital world. Cyber Dust allows the user to send private, encrypted, disappearing messages to friends or coworkers. I even sent a message to Mark and received almost an immediate reply to my question.

VSCO Cam
iOS / Android

VSCO Cam in my opinion is the best built-in camera app. Featuring the top notch shooting and editing tools with plenty of filters to try out.

FireChat
iOS / Android

FireChat is a messaging app that works without 3G or Wi-Fi, using a network created by the devices around you. This is great for traveling with friends, as well as sports and music events.

Productivity

Slack
iOS / Android / Windows Phone
Slack is a messaging service for your work desktop and mobile. It's a quick way to contact colleagues. Making it perfect for reducing your email inbox clutter.

Wunderlist
iOS / Android / Windows Phone
Another team productivity app like Freedcamp. Microsoft bought Wunderlist is a to-do list app for individual tasks to complicated projects.

IF by IFTTT
iOS / Androids
This is a wonderful way to connect all your other apps and automate the tasks that go between them. You can upload your photos to Dropbox and save important articles you want to read later on.

Mailbox
iOS / Android
Tired of a ton of crap in your Inbox? This is the most useful tool for bringing the number of emails in your inbox to Zero. You swipe emails out of your inbox, including making some return later at a time of your choice. I personally use this for my gmail account but it's also available for Icloud.

Scanner Pro 6 by Readdle
iOS

Whether you're having to print and sign PDF documents before returning them digitally, or simply keeping digital copies of documents and receipts, this app is the best option.

1Password
iOS / Android

1Password stores all of your login passwords and username details. The information is also encrypted, keeping your information safe.

Dropbox
iOS / Android / Windows Phone
Similar to Google Drive, Dropbox performs the same function. Allowing you to auto upload your videos and images to you the cloud system. I personally can not speak upon the qaulity

Travel

Microsoft Translator
iOS / Android / Windows Phone
This app is one of my own personal favorites. It will translate words and phrases while you're traveling the world. It features over 40 different languages and the coolest part about this Microsoft translator. Is that it gives you the option to have things read out or displayed on screen for you to try the the language featured on the application.

Hotel Tonight
iOS / Android / Windows Phone

You get a call suddenly or you're doing well financially, you decide to take a last minute trip leaving you with almost no time to book your accommodations. You pull out your smartphone and you book your accommodations for the night right there.

TripCase

This app allows users to organize multiple flights, hotel reservations and plans. Most importantly, you're able to follow along with each other's, allowing families or friends to be updated on your travels. If your flight is delayed or changed, notifications are automatically shared with your family or friends. They can keep tabs on you, making a great app to not only travel but to let your family know you're safe at all times.

Local Eats
iOS

The app also allows you to request a taxi cab ride to your desired restaurant. It's a great app featuring only independently owned restaurants. Giving the user an authentic taste of the culture their visiting, this is usually the first app I open anytime I'm in a new country or city.

Chapter 3: Facebook Famous

Facebook Is literally the perfect app to assist you while building your empire. It allows you to build the perfect network. For the sake of the importance of this topic, I've broken it up into 2 chapters. Facebook has played such a role in my success that I feel it's the most effective tool for the construction of your online business. In my experience, Facebook Networking can literally be life or death when it comes to your business success. It's not enough to simply have a skill, it's about who you know. As I sit here and type this very paragraph, I'm intoxicated by success. I may not drive a Ferrari, I may not own a Yacht but the success I've experienced, big and small has not come from being the most talented, the smartest or the best looking. My success has 90% been contributed to who I know and not what I can do, this is mainly attributed to my relationships on Facebook.

Introduction to success

The following information will be broken into simple steps. By the end of this chapter you will learn.

Friend Request: You feel your phone vibrate in your pocket while you are at the movie theater watching the movie Dead pool with a few of your buddies. You whip out your phone and see that a man named Thomas Blanc has sent you a friend request, you accept his request and put your phone away so you can continue to enjoy the latest hollywood blockbuster. Exactly one hour and 45 minutes later, you get home and decide to scroll down your news feed. You see in the top right corner of your screen that you have 12 new notifications. You click the notifications icon and realize that Thomas Blanc without introducing himself has stalked you on facebook for exactly the last one hour and 45 minutes. Thomas has liked several of your pictures, stupid memes and post but he's yet to have introduced himself. You'd think that if he was so interested in connecting with you, he'd at least shoot you a quick message introducing himself right? You brush it off, think not much of it and go back to bed. 3 days go by and Thomas is still virtually stalking you without giving you an introduction. Even worse, the asshole has the nerve to leave a comment on one of your statuses expressing his disapproval in your opinion. "Seriously, who the hell is this guy"? you think to yourself. Finally you've had enough and you either send him a quick message saying "Hey, where do I know you from"? Or if you're like me, you block and delete this internet creep and hopefully lose him for good.

The best part about social media is that it connects you to people from all over the world. It' doesn't matter who you are, you'll always find other people who share the same ideas, hobbies and opinions as you do. Most Often these people will reach out to you and send you a friend request. The worst part about social media is people actually seem to forget that there is an actual real person on the other end of the computer screen. You can't just walk around telling people you like them in real life, asking them to be your friend and most importantly, publicly express your disapproval on your review of the most awesome movie ever created (DeadPool Starring Ryan Reynolds, who by the way is not nearly as handsome as the guy writing this paragraph) without ever giving some kind of an introduction right? So why is it people feel that they can do the same thing on social media? Wouldn't it be weird if someone came up to you one day on the street and said, "I overheard you say maple syrup is delicious on bacon but i'm here to tell you just how wrong you truly are" Like who does that? Oh, and in case you're wondering? Maple syrup on bacon is absolutely wonderful, I suggest you try it.

The first hello: Let's face it, anyone can be on the other end of that screen. So when you're reaching out to other people on facebook and sending them freinds request it's important that you message them as soon as possible. You' could be a stalker/serial killer waiting to kill them and wear their skin for all they know. So making an introduction is important but it's no longer good enough to just send a simple text message to their inbox.

Here are 3 ways you can introduce yourself to your new facebook buddy.

1.The most common way is by sending them a text message directly to their inbox. This is by far the most outdated and stupid way to say hello. Who actually trust anyone on the internet anymore? I'm pretty sure we can all agree serial killer stalkers who wear their victim's skin pretty much ruined this for all of us. If you're still doing this I recommended you stop immediately, you're more likely freaking people out. This person isn't even sure if they can trust you.They've yet to confirm that you are the person in your profile picture so why would they be interested in you messaging them to tell them about your product, service or anything at all? Once again, stop text introductions immediately.

2. Voice Messaging: One of my favourite handy little tools on the facebook messaging app. It allows the option to record a 60 second voice clips and immediately send it off. Not only is this easier to communicate what you're trying to say but unless you sound like famous actor James Earl Jones (Darth Vader) it actually comes across as extremely thoughtful and not creepy. However, until you actually have communicated regularly with this person and they become sure that they can trust you, or at the very least you're not the stalker/serial killer I had mentioned earlier. This still isn't good enough for making a real introduction.

3. Video Introduction: This is the most important step in your introduction. As soon as you send a request or accept a request, it's important that you send them a quick video introduction. Even if it's as simple as a hello. This not only allows you to make a good impression but allows them to know you're someone they can trust. Think about it, if you're willing to blast your face out there you probably don't have too much to hide right? At Least the chances of you being a creepo or serial killer stalker has greatly decreased. However, sending a video just to say hello and building a valuable network that will benefit you in the long run are 2 diffrent things.

Here's what a valuable introduction should sound and look like: For starters, you need to have a shirt on, be in a clean room with decent lighting and you need to speak loud and clear, no stuttering, drawn out pauses or "Ummms". Do not hit the send button until your video and presentation is the highest quality you possibly can come up with given your speaking abilities and camera quality at the time. It's doesn't have to be the best video, just be specific to the point. The goal isn't to produce an epic/edited introduction video, the goal is to be considerate and professional. You want to come across as if you actually value and acknowledge them as another human being. This is how you leave a lasting impact on another individual. I believe it was Jim Carey who said "The greatest currency is how we make others feel" I truly believe that statement.

That's how you give a proper Facebook Introduction.

Building Relationships

The most Beautiful part about facebook's is it's ability to allow yourself to build a real lasting friendship or romantic relationship with an actual human being and not just their business. The majority of other social media platforms are not only less interactive but they are less personal. Facebook has not only given me many of my most valuable business relationships and friendships , but facebook allowed me to find and soon marry my bribe to be who actually lived in another country. You better start building those relationships now. It's important you notice how I said "relationships" and not followers. All this and more will be talked about in this chapter.

What it means to build a relationship

Everyone knows what a relationship is but do they know what it means to truly have one?

A relationship between people is something that's formed from a repetitive introduction. Each person is re introduced to one another until the 2 or more people accept each other person as a part of their reality. This means your coworkers and even family members had to learn to accept you as a part of their reality before getting use to your presence. Being apart of someone's reality in a way is becoming apart of a tribe. No you don't have to like them but people will have to encounter each other to solve some type of problem your tribe may be attempting to solve in that period of time. The relationship you build with others is mostly based off of the problem you solve for each other or as a group. This is the very foundation all relationships are built off of.

Value: When discussing value it's important that you understand we're talking about people, not houses or any other property. I'm talking about the nature of the person, the way they think, their lifestyle, their religion and their talents. These are some of the many things and that make up the human character. You are the one who decides the right combination of unique characteristics that makes a person valuable to you. These values must align with yours and yours align with theirs. It's not a one way streak, the person who has the most value is the person who is willing to give as much as they have even if they do not have the most to offer. It's the intention in which we give, that matters most in our relationships. However this does not mean you can't lose value in your relationships. Losing value to people happens everyday in human interactions. It's important that we constantly evaluate ourselves, mainly for us and not just the other person.

The Process Of Re-evaluation

Relationships are tricky, they can deteriorate easier than they can be built. Relationships breakdown usually for one reason, neglect. It is in my humblest opinion that neglect is the killer of all relationships. Neglect in the relationships first starts when you stop taking care of yourself and your business. To take care of your relationships you must first take care of yourself. Nothing positive can come out of any relationship when we aren't handling our own shit. It's impossible to be valuable to others when your life is a complete disaster. Can you imagine having to carry someone on a broken leg? You wouldn't be able to do it and that's what it's like trying to help other people when your own life is in a disaster. This is the number one reason we constantly re evaluate our own personal progress on our life's purpose. We don't want to let those we care about down. nothing in my eyes is more important than that.

How to re evaluate yourself

Honesty: Is not only the first step but the hardest when it come to improving yourself. I have never met a single person who is 100% honest with themselves, 100% of the time. Honesty is the very foundation which supports yours change and your growth throughout your life, it's the only reason we can change and become more than what we are. Nothing is more powerful than looking yourself in the mirror and being honest with yourself about every aspect of your life.

Relationships Before Money

Everyone wants money, everyone needs money. So believe me when I tell you that my intention in this chapter isn't to downplay the importance for money. The problem is when you put more importance on money instead of relationships, it's next to impossible to bring money in consistently. Money is accumulated on the foundation of relationships. The relationships of your staff, your partners, your customers and yourself. How can you have a return customer if your relationship is not just unestablished but is left in a negative outlook after their first and last interaction with you?

When just getting started you have 3 objectives

1. Building the most powerful network you possibly can

2. Selecting at least 5 people who you feel could benefit from building a relationship with you and communicate with them at least once a week. Doing this consistently builds trust and all stable relationships are built from trust. Slowly you'll expand your circle more but to be sure to communicate with at least 5 people a day online to appear more trustworthy.

3. Help them or work for them for free. I'm not saying to do this forever but the best way to build a relationship with another human being, is to help solve a problem. Problem solving for free will not only serve them but it will serve you 10x more in the long run. It's hard to be recommended if you're constantly proposing offers but yet not closing any deals. This is especially important when first starting out in any area of expertise. No one, myself included is willing to give money to anyone who isn't willing to do at least one thing to help solve their problem until they've seen how this person can fix his or her unique problem.

Chapter 4: To Catch And Kill A Catfish

No, I'm not talking about the ugly Marine animal. I'm talking about someone who is a creepy asshole. According to the urban dictionary.com.

"A catfish is someone who pretends to be someone they're not, using Facebook or other social media to create false identities, particularly to pursue deceptive online romances.

Did you hear how Dave got totally catfished last month? The fox he thought he was talking to turned out to be a pervy guy from San Diego!

or

I was really falling for that gorgeous gal on Facebook, but she turned out to be a catfish"

Much creepier than you thought eh? It's estimated between 67.65 million and 137.76 million accounts on Facebook are either duplicates or false. The sad part is Facebook isn't 100 sure of the exact number.

You can't speak of the benefits of networking online without discussing its downfalls. Besides falling victim for internet marketing schemes, Cat fishing is possibly the most real and most dangerous threat out there. A catfish with too much information can be the very person who could end up stealing thousands and possibly millions if they are knowledgeable enough to do so. Presenting themselves as friends, associates with similar or even potential business partners. Catch fishes are the Trojan horses of the internet. Every friend request could potentially be an enemy waiting to breach your walls and cause as much damage from the inside out as possible. Whether it's to use your personal photos, steal and sell your personal or professional information. Or who knows, maybe it's a person you already know pretending to be someone else to fulfill whatever sick agenda they have planned. These assholes have nothing but bad intentions for you, learning how to find catch a catfish and kill one isn't necessarily important but is definitely fun. The worst part about it is Facebook does not know how many fake profiles are out there.

Here's a very true story, but first let me state that the names of the characters mentioned are changed to protect their true identity.

Once upon a time was a beautiful 19-year-old teen girl named Corrina Kelly. Corrina Kelly was the finest dame in all the land. Corrina was 5'4 had blonde hair, almost crystal clear blue eyes, gorgeous dimples and a perfect smile. Corrina was fine alright, and her man was a 6-foot tall giant named Wayne Jordan. You see, Wayne was a ladies man, he had great social skills, very well educated and overall an interesting character. In fact, both Corrina and Wayne had hundreds of like on all their facebook statuses and constantly posted enlightening and complicated topics that would definitely make you appreciate both their level of intelligence. Time went on and Wayne seemed to create a macro level of facebook fame for himself, Life was good for Mr. Jordan. He was getting all the social media validation he ever wanted, but something just wasn't right. Slowly I started to notice a few patterns between Wayne and Corrina's Facebook statuses. He and Corrina not only sounded similar but exactly the same. At first I just thought maybe I was being paranoid, but I later found out I wasn't the only one who felt this way. Usually a creepo on social media creating multiple accounts just to get social validation is completely harmless and defiantly didn't affect my personal or offline life in anyway shape or form. Unfortunately for hundreds of other men I can not say the same.

Corrina Kelly contacted a person who is in a very famous book and who was very well known in the men's self-improvement community online. This semi-famous individual showed her picture to a friend of mine who apparently knew Wayne was a fraud the whole time but didn't say anything, believing Wayne was harmless at the time. Corrina Kelly in reality, was not Corrina Kelly, she was Wayne Jordan. Shortly after, Wayne was publicly called out, humiliated and exposed for the fraud he was. Now, you're probably wondering "Why it matters so much that Wayne was pretending to be a creepo on facebook"?

Wayne's crime was not fulfilling his fantasy of being a 5'4 blonde babe. Wayne's crime was what he did to hundreds of men posing as Corrina Kelly. It was exposed that Wayne under the facebook avatar Corrina Kelly was seducing men online, soliciting them for money, getting them to send him dick pics and he even admitted to selling those online and using them as blackmail against anyone who caught onto his act. It's said many of these men were his own clients from his internet dating business but these claims have not been admitted by Wayne.

The purpose of this chapter is to remind everyone of the dangers on social media. It's great having access to any community of like-minded individuals whom you can share your ideas and opinions with at just a click of a button. Unfortunately not all of us are simply interested in building a valuable relationship or network. On every platform and in every group is hundreds of fake profiles, many of which are likely created by the same person. Your job isn't to seek out the catfish but to never give up to much personal information to anyone you meet online, even if you end up meeting them in person. A few people Wayne targeted online he had actually met offline and started building a relationship with those individuals under the identity Corrina Kelly.

Confirming they are who they claim to be is no longer enough. I believe knowing their intentions for contacting and networking with you is the most important of all. If someone adds you on facebook or any other social media platforms without sending you a brief bio of who they are, what they do and why they felt the need to add you to social media. Send them a message and find out. If you don't get a response within 24 hours, block and delete them immediately. They could be stealing your pictures, along with any other available information you have posted on your profile for your friends to see.

Now that you've caught the catfish, the next step is to kill the catfish. I shouldn't have to say this but with the level of stupidity people seem to possess, I will.

"Do Not Literally Kill Anyone, This Is A Metaphor"

Now that we have that out of the way here are a few steps you can take to get rid of the catfish the properly.

1. Screen shot any evidence from conversations you may have had with this person incase you need it to validate your claim.

2. Publicly expose them for being a fraud: The best way to do this is by creating a post with their image, a screenshot of evidence supporting your claim and tag them and all of your mutual friends in this post. You never want to find out this kind of information and allow this catfish to potentially steal information or sabotage others if you can somehow warn other people of their activity.

3. Next, report the false profile to facebook and get your mutual friends to do the same. Also, keep in mind that their is a strong possibility that 2 or more of your mutual friends could possibly be the same individual since people who cat fish usually have multiple profiles.

Chapter 5 - How To Make Your Post More visible on Facebook

. Don't Be An Attention Whore

Avoid asking friends or followers to like, share or comment on your post. Facebook recently had an algorithm change to weed out post that look like spam.

. Get your friends or followers to like, share or comment on your post.

Posting things your friends care about actually helps feed the algorithm which allows your friends to see your post more frequently. Start by posting trendy topics, the more likes you get the more people will see. As long as you focus on getting your content in front of more eyeballs you shouldn't have a problem with getting likes organically, without having to beg for them.

. Start a Conversation

If you can get a conversation started with a post by asking a question, it's more likely your Page will be pulled into other people's feeds. Make sure the question are either relevant to your business or are on trendy topics. Offensive topics can get attention however this attention could easily turn against you so be careful.

Target Your Posts

If you're not an expert at marketing no worries. Now on Facebook you're given the ability to target Page posts to specific users based on their age, gender, location, relationship status, interest, needs, keywords and other options. If a person is a pitbull lover and you're selling "I love Pitbulls" T-shirts? Facebook ad targeting has been the most effective way in my own personal experience to reach new customers.

Avoid openly angry or opinionated post.

In 2013 Facebook conducted a controversial experiment. Manipulating the news feed to measure people's moods when they saw an abundance of negative or positive post. Facebook found that users who saw more positive posts were more likely to share. The company has incorporated that experiment into its algorithm. So it's important and beneficial for everyone to post positive topics instead of conspiracy propaganda or anything that could cause a negative emotion.

Post at Odd Hours

Now 787 million people are now visiting Facebook every day, you want to try posting at different times everyday. The great thing about facebook is that you can setup your page to post at many different times throughout the day. A great habit to have before bed is setting several different post to be released throughout the night while you sleep and early morning for before you wake up and an hour after you typically wake up.

Be Engaging

The best way to build an engaging audience, offer relevant content that attracts user engagement. Not only that but it's important you don't play shy. People have taken the time to comment, like and share their opinions on your post which contributes to your visibility. Take the time to comment back, let them see that there is a real person on the other side of the monitor. Also don't be afraid to respectfully disagree, debate or take sides. It's so uncommon for that to happen that your audience will definitely respond well to your engagement and continue to engage back. Invite others to the conversation which helps grow your audience.

Cross-Promote With Other Pages

Again, this goes back to building relationships with other people. Contact an admin of a page you fell aligns with your values. Discuss with them your interest in what they offer and negotiate a cross promotion between the two of you and make it fair as possible.

Chapter 6 - Live Video Streams

From rehearsals to announcements, live streaming is the future. Look around, we all have a camera wherever we go. With the mobile device in your pocket and the new trend of live streaming. Anyone can become a journalist or an actor. We have countless of video platforms allowing people to instantly hear whatever it is you have to say within a matter of seconds. This is only further proof of just how powerful the smartphone has become.

Here are the top 3 streaming services you must use right away.

Facebook: As if facebook wasn't already a force to be reckoned with, they've added their own streaming feature allowing you to broadcast live at a click of button.

Periscope: Periscope is a smartphone app available for Android and iOS systems, which allows users to access live-streaming video from around the world. It was created by Kayvon Beykpour and Joe Bernstein and was later on picked up by Twitter for $100 million. I've seen users broadcast things from puppet shows to live streaming apple product launch announcements. Periscope is not only fun, but is a valuable tool for people who are creative and are willing to try new things with their smartphone camera.

Youtube: As you can imagine the people who benefit the most from live streaming features are youtuber who've been building their channels for years. Many of which have hit a million or more subscribers.

To Be Continued………..

And that ladies and gentlemen is the introduction to the basics of building a Smartphone Empire. I gave you everything to get started but this is only the beginning. I will be releasing part 2 on May 30th.

If you're interested in part 2 of this series please send me an email books4abetterlife@gmail.com with the subject "Smartphone Empire" and I'll be sure to send you free copy.

www.ingramcontent.com/pod-product-compliance
Lightning Source LLC
Chambersburg PA
CBHW080528190526
45169CB00008B/3093